SPONTANEOUS COMBUSTIONS

SPONTANEOUS COMBUSTIONS
57 Non-Haikus followed by
California Raisins

Seb Doubinsky

LEAKY BOOT PRESS

*Spontaneous Combustions: 57 Non-Haikus
followed by California Raisins*
by Seb Doubinsky

First published in 2014 by
Leaky Boot Press
http://www.leakyboot.com

Copyright © 2014 Seb Doubinsky
All rights reserved

No part of this book may be reproduced or transmitted in any form or by any means, electronic, mechanical, photocopying, recording, or otherwise, without prior written permission of the author.

ISBN: 978-1-909849-07-5

Contents

Non–Autumn	9
Non–Winter	33
Non–Spring	47
Non–Summer	61
California Raisins	77

To Matt B., Matt R. and Matt G.

NON-AUTUMN

1

drizzle drizzle drizzle
taking the kids to school
head empty of all thoughts
—fatherhood

2

fistfight
shock of knuckles against a jaw
smell of stale sweat, beer and stupid blood
—ah poetry

3

they predicted rain
the sun is playing on my lawn
—the tragedy of life

4

children panic when
they can't find things
at the same spot
—Adults don't
although they should

5

flash-floods in the night
—20,000 lightnings
but no illumination

6

painted clouds
on a painted sky
—only my hangover seems real

7

to stut
ter
is
to be
come
lan
guage

8

what we think we remember:
a book a film a kiss a girl a boy
what we actually remember:
ourselves
remembering

9

this poem
is two minutes late
—the coffee stands still

10

spontaneity is key
—the cat yawns
and jumps on the kitchen table

11

white day
smell of rubbing alcohol
—uncertainties of the heart

12

discussing literature
in my colleague's office
—the sun ignores us

13

language
speaks
language
—no noise

14

this teddy-bear misses one eye,
one arm and reeks of old snot
—the kid is growing

15

a bird flies
into a cloud
—I disappear

16

the meeting goes on
the system wants us to be mowed down with grace
I look at the ceiling to avoid looking at my watch
—suddenly autumn

17

in the bus
the prof reads his book
the poet looks at the landscape
—both working

18

there will be no
poets this year
—go home

19

poems hate you
—eat shit and die

20

The poetry shall not be televised
—it shall be lived

21

smoke in my lungs
—I cough
my ghost

22

autumn clearance sale
—everything must go
including you

NON-WINTER

23

the evening chill
reminds us that our bones
are made of glass

24

we wish all things would be eternal
yet we always forget to buy the sugar

25

the sun, the wheel and a grey sky
—I wonder what card
I should play

26

winter
—icy fog creeping
like forgotten love letters

27

foggy window
clear mind
—winter can come

28

watching tv without watching
breathing without thinking
—winter has settled in

29

the sun shines in the cold air
a silent bird swings on a branch
—blue winter, green soul

30

no poems for christmas
no poems to open up like presents
no colourful paper to fill up the garbage-can

31

I won't write another stupid poem
about the beauty of snow
—the blue sky freezes my words

32

regrets of greens and yellows
of salty mist on the forehead
and no shoes to wear
—the easy sentimentality of winter

33

inspiration
expiration
—the span
of the poet's life

NON-SPRING

34

the homeless man
takes off his coat
and puts it next to him
on the pavement
—spring

35

the sun slowly rises over the roofs
a bird sings, then stops

36

chilly grey day
—even the birds
don't pretend to be birds

37

the yellowed leaves
are jumping back
into the book
—spring

38

Rimbaud's shop sign
flashes glamorously
over the sidewalk:
"An I for an I"
—poetic deals 7/24

39

a scent of earth, grass and sunshine
an empty chair and discarded shoes
—spring has just left the room

40

a plane on the window-pane
—flatness of the eye

41

words never fail
lips, tongue and mouth do
but breath is always to blame

42

non-spring is the non-season of non-love
—a leaf falls before its time

43

a rose is a rose
but not a rose

44

heavy clouds over the garden
—today spring is more a poem
than a season

NON-SUMMER

45

the swimming pool evaporates
under the flat round sun
and my words dissolve
like blinding icecubes

46

does the bird
that sings in the tree
know that I am not there?

47

light is as flat as it is deep
—quiet thoughts under
the shadow of a tree

48

let's sing a song
before we die
—my bones rattle
like drums
in the darkness
of the bar

49

my age at some point
remembered through poetry
—I wonder if its hair will change color

50

flowers blossom on the stairs
the cat purrs in the shade
words become smells
and drift away

51

poems fuck who they want
—poems are not poets

52

poetry is both wave and particle

53

I cannot describe what I see
I can only evoke its movement
—a motel by the side of the road

54

small ganesh,
buddha and batmobile
on my desk
life as objects
words in the making

55

inspiration is an illusion

56

summer is the season of perspectives
will it rain? will you love me forever?

57

a season passes
a new season begins
the poet ages faster
than the grass he mows

CALIFORNIA RAISINS

Dedicated to
Christina Mesa

California Raisins

Nothing original here, California raisins
White teeth, paper smiles
Americans gulp gas by the gallon
—souls on sale, two for the price of one
You know a good deal when you see one

(Gee-whizz! This one's a winner!)

And yet—smartass Frenchman
Good deal, my ass! Mexican fat asses, Black fat asses, Jewish
Fat asses, Asian fat asses, Caucasian fat asses
—"Happy, happy" not "happy"
Nothing original here, California raisins

(Garbageland in between CalTrain tracks
—Abundance is for everyone)

And yet—melancholic Kerouac fog
Memories of dust and tar at dusk
A symphony somewhere
Bursts out from the copper clouds
Nothing original here, California raisins

(Faces blur as we pass them, blue eyes
Floating alone on a shimmering flag)

And yet—I am waiting for my wife
In Macy's, sitting next to a tanned
And very depressed man
Sofie is buying a pair of jeans (on sale)
size 12 short she has just discovered
I wonder if the same sizes apply for coffins
Nothing original here, California raisins

(You want candy? I've got candy!
You want teeth too?)

And yet—you cannot park here
In the land of signs and warnings
And long poems
Old Whitmanian trembling hands
On the computer's keyboard
Nothing original here, California raisins

(A police siren ejaculates in my ear,
My deflowered eardrum bleeds)

And yet—all Americans are monsters
Great laughter gushing out of'
Their humongous lungs
Gargantuan bellies, Mount
Rushmore heads
Nothing original here, California raisins

(Does my voice annoy you? Should
I strum a guitar instead and hum?)

And yet—poems! I dry cough
My words in the Californian cold
Soul shirts hanging still

In the lethal blue sky
Made in China
Nothing original here, California raisins

(The poet is traditionally either
A social outcast or a pain in the ass)

And yet—fragments,
Fragments, fragments
Of my sonic Paly High youth,
Pimply youth, imaginary youth,
Youth youth
Nothing original here, California Raisins

(Hey, youth, keep off my "I can't believe it's not lawn" lawn!)

(Ad-lib isn't poetry they say, but then what is?)

And yet—chilly San Francisco streets
Steep as Afghan mountains, the crazy cackle
Of Falungong fanatics screaming "Scum! Scum! Scum!"
At the top of their yellowed lungs
Melting teapot in the rising cotton fog
Nothing original here, California Raisins

(Sofie hides to smoke cigarettes—her lungs
Blacken and glow in the shadow)

And yet—riding the Sandburg trains
Alongside square bungalows
And empty car dealer lots
Because people don't
Get repaired here

They're just discarded
And replaced
Nothing original here, California raisins

(So easy to be critical, but real hearts beat
Under the plastic, I'm sure)

And yet—bluebirds, squirrels and raccoons
Sunny side up on the flat freeways
Organic death trip to cure you from
The joys of age and experience
Nothing original here, California raisins

(Displaced country music intermezzo)

And yet—48 going on 49, last time
Here in 1983, everything has changed
But me, nothing has changed but me
A question of perspective
Under the moon's silvery fish-hook
Nothing original here, California raisins

(City Lights Book Inc., where
Are the snows of yesterday?)

And yet—Hispanic teenage families
Whispering threats and lovewords
To each other while bouncing the
Next generation on their miserable knees
(*Te quiero mucho, hijo de puta*)
Baseball caps and heavy makeup
Made of dreams and sorrows
All wrapped-up like beautiful candy
Nothing original here, California raisins

(Still the wind sings and carries
Wonderful news to the seagulls)

And yet—a red wheelbarrow comes
Crashing down the street and fate
Deals its cards on route 84
But who is afraid of the shadows of the trees?
Nothing original here, California raisins

(A friend of the devil is a friend of mine)

And yet—Richard Brautigans's old dungarees
Hung to dry somewhere
On a rusty clothesline
In a forgotten barn half eaten
By yellow grass and morning glories
Nothing original here, California raisins

(Poems are mental constructions
Reflecting our mental constructions)

And yet—non-haikus chirping
On the redwood branches
Like non-birds
Reminiscence of nature
Once felt and never forgotten
Yet never felt again in the same
Forgotten way
Nothing original here, California raisins

(And yet)

And yet—I met Yevtushenko again
In San Gregorio, I don't know why

But I always meet him in dark American
Bookstores, he always has a friendly smile
And a frank communist handshake
Red words black words yellow words
One star, one hope
One bear also
Sipping tea pouring out
Of a silver samovar
Nothing original here, California raisins

(My father's silhouette standing in a corner
Of the Stanford-in-Tours library
Turning pages and smiling as he reads—from here,
It looks like one of my books—of course, this is
Only a dream)

And yet—back in Half Moon Bay
Where a lot of all this started in 1983
Two drunken Mexican women
Are dancing together in the mild chipotle wind
To the tinny music of a five dollar radio
Hermosas frutas de California
Nothing original here, California raisins

(Memories melt under the sun to harden again in the colder days)

And yet—some say that poetry is photorealistic
But I don't know—my images are made out of
Safeway brown bags and Gucci shoeboxes
A collage of bills, vintage postcards and love letters
Held together by sweat and coffee rings
Nothing original here, California raisins

(This is a safe place)

And yet—this poem is not improvised
But very slowly constructed like a card tower
A castle made of matches or a relationship
Gotta watch out for the wind
Or for the children's sudden gestures
What you see on the floor is part
Of the poem too—dust, feathers, tears
Nothing original here, California raisins

(Some say that sorrow has the size of the heart,
But that joy fills the whole body)

(I don't know about that, though)

(But it fits well into this poem)

And yet—nice conversation with strangers
In the Wharf's "In-N-Out" burger restaurant
Renegade Mormon couple explaining to us
The three different types of Mormon heaven
They told us you had to pay
To enter the last one—no wonder Vegas
Is in Holy Nevada
Nothing original here, California raisins

(We crossed the blue streets of San Francisco
Without climbing a single hill—the Saint
Of Streetcars was watching over us)

And yet—Power believes in magic
That's why there are so many signs
By the side of the sidewalks and roads

It believes that words can control
—And this is why: silence
Nothing original here, California raisins

(American Standard)

And yet—sweet Christina, and her beautiful son Thor
Handsome like a dark thunder god,
And Snowball the cat with the perfectly round eyes
Californian nonchalance and deep red beating hearts
Radiating music and loved memories
Nothing original here, California Raisins

(Even in the darkness I can see her smile)

(And yet)

And yet—flat Los Angeles surrounded by hills
Hunched like the backs of defeated buffaloes
Electronic mantras by the side of the pool
Amitoba ne répond plus
Matt and Nicole humming deconstructed songs
In the car while Eric curls his ironic lips
In the smoggy sunset
Poets and musicians eternally bound
By melodies and the price of gas
Nothing original here, California raisins

(There was a chase on the 101, then the guys got into an accident, but left their vehicle on foot. They were later found hiding in an apartment. Helicopters buzzed over our heads like aggressive bees)

And yet—Athanasius Kirchner in the small museum

The theory of everything and more right under
Our peering eyes—some explanations are missing
And some of the exhibitions are broken
But no matter—all roads lead to Rome
And a good hanging
Nothing original here, California raisins

(I have a book on Kirchner at home, which I bought some twenty years ago. Poets think they're alchemists when they truly are unbeknownst chemists)

And yet—slight Bukowski hangover
Clouds hanging low over the skyline
Miles and miles of concrete walls,
Stucco façades and cracked swimming pools
Many minotaurs are hiding in the shopping malls
While a few matadors drive by in their low-riders
I can see the monsters but who are the heroes?
Huge shape in the clouds dissolving in grey haze
Nothing original here, California raisins

(When we die doesn't matter—it's how we die that does)

(If astrology could tell us that, nobody would want to know)

(One palm reading, 10$ Two palms 15$)

(If you're a monkey, you get a 50% discount)

And yet—riding the Venice wave
Barefoot in grey fog, sand and concrete
Our shadows folded in our pockets
Wet and speckled with wall paint
Nothing original here, California raisins

(My voice is not my voice, this poem is not my poem
Yet my voice is my voice and this poem is my poem
—this is to help future students and readers)

And yet—memories pile on memories
Like water on water or wind on wind
California rebuilt anew from the ruins
In my soul—poetry is the strongest earthquake
Of all earthly earthquakes—it can shake up
The stars too and a few good teeth
Nothing original here, California raisins

(And yet, and yet)

You know a good deal when you see one
—souls on sale, two for the price of one
Americans gulp gas by the gallons
White teeth, paper smiles
Nothing original here, California raisins

San Francisco—Los Angeles
June 2012

More Poetry & Lyrics From
Leaky Boot Press

Mothballs: Quantum Poems
Seb Doubinsky

Mothballs: Quantum Poems is the long awaited new collection by the internationally acclaimed poet Seb Doubinsky.

"The whole collection... reads as one long poem with pauses in between (the white noise of daily life) and then these snapshots of sheer magic that radiate with a synaesthesia of all the senses intermingling- words, breath, the ticking of the clock. There is such a pulse in these lines..."

Cynthia Atkins, author of
Psyche's Weathers and *In the Event of Full Disclosure*

ISBN: 978-1-909849-00-6

The Kindest Lies: the Lyrics of John Lyle
John Lyle

Reading like the best kind of poetry—moving, emotive, wistful, relevant and often funny—the lyrics of Canadian singer-songwriter John Lyle throw our world and our lives into sharp focus.

Not but a shadow
Hold my world of stormy care

There is never time to waste in this holy place, which is this land we live in. This life, this vast landscape of the heart. Those are John's words and Woody would concur and so would all of the great poets. The valley might be lonesome and the blossoms might be broken but to John Lyle they will always scent the morning air. Always. And to me, this lies at the heart of John's art.

Matt Bialer, author of *Bridge*

ISBN: 978-1-909849-01-3

More Poetry & Lyrics From
Leaky Boot Press

Nothing is Complete Before it is Broken
Ole Wesenberg Nielsen

The new collection of poems in the English language by an admired Danish poet.

Seb Ole Wesenberg Nielsen is a Danish punk poet whose work is widely admired.

"Ole Wesenberg Nielsen's poems question our smug, self-satisfied society. . . nothing is safe from the stiletto jabs of his words as they attack the flesh of cant, hypocrisy and self-delusion."

ISBN: 978-1-909849-02-0

Bridge
Matt Bialer

Vanished civilizations, unidentified flying objects, giant people, strange sea creatures, alien visitations, enigmatic ancient artifacts. . . Government conspiracies, media fraudsters, mass hysteria, genuine believers. . . Welcome to the world of Matt Bialer. A fascination with the strange, the unexplained and the downright weird manifests itself hypnotically in this selection of long poems that address our hopes, our misconceptions and our fears about things we don't understand. These poems read like fast paced stories, never fail to entertain.

"These poems are the epic celebration of Americana at its weirdest, an elegy to the beauty of its deeply twisted and beautiful soul. Amazing."

Seb Doubinsky author of
Spontaneous Combustions, Mothballs, Absinth & The Song of Synth
and *The Babylonian Trilogy*

ISBN: 978-1-909849-04-4

www.ingramcontent.com/pod-product-compliance
Lightning Source LLC
LaVergne TN
LVHW091315080426
835510LV00007B/504